CULLEN **BUNN** JESÚS **HERVÁS** NIKO **GUARDIA**

THE EMPTY MAN™

MANIFESTATION

THE EMPTY MAN: Manifestation, November 2019. Published by BOOM! Studios, a division of Boom Entertainment, Inc.

BOOM! Studios, 5670 Wilshire Boulevard, Suite 400, Los Angeles, CA, 90036-5679. Printed in China. First Printing.

ISBN: 978-1-68415-431-9, eISBN: 978-1-64144-548-1

RESTRICTED
AREA

THE
EMPTY
MAN
MANIFESTATION
™

WRITTEN BY CULLEN BUNN
ILLUSTRATED BY JESÚS HERVÁS
COLORED BY NIKO GUARDIA
LETTERED BY ED DUKESHIRE
COVER BY VANESA R. DEL REY
SERIES DESIGNER MARIE KRUPINA
COLLECTION DESIGNER JILLIAN CRAB
EDITOR ERIC HARBURN
SPECIAL THANKS MATTHEW LEVINE & CHRIS ROSA
THE EMPTY MAN CREATED BY CULLEN BUNN

CHAPTER ONE

HRRK

RRRK?

SPLISH

RRRK?

...WE STILL DON'T HAVE MANY DETAILS ABOUT **WHAT** OCCURRED HERE IN THE EARLY HOURS OF THE MORNING...
...BUT WE HAVE RECEIVED REPORTS OF GUNSHOTS, SCREAMING, AND OTHER LOUD DISTURBANCES.
WE CAN SEE SIGNS OF VIOLENCE, INCLUDING SHATTERED WINDOWS AND EVEN BLOOD ON THE PAVEMENT.

"CONSIDERING THE NEIGHBORHOOD-WIDE MASSACRE THAT OCCURRED JUST A FEW MILES AWAY..."
OH MY GOD--
"...EARLY SPECULATION IS THAT THIS INCIDENT IS ALSO CONNECTED TO THE **EMPTY MAN VIRUS**."

WHAT IS **THAT?**

WE'VE GOT EVERYTHING COVERED IN HERE, OFFICERS.
I NEED YOU OUTSIDE.
MAKE SURE THE CIVILIANS STAY ON THE OTHER SIDE OF THE BARRICADE.

YES, SIR.

OREO
WE NEED TO GET THIS WRAPPED UP.
LAST THING WE NEED IS FOR SOMEONE TO CATCH A GLIMPSE OF...
...WHATEVER THE HELL THAT IS!

YOU HEARD THE MAN.
COME ON.

AMEN.

EMERGENCY
THIS MAN'S BEEN INJURED!
HE NEEDS HELP! RIGHT AWAY!

WE NEED *HELP!*

OH...OH, MY...
WHAT HAPPENED TO HIM?
HE WAS... ATTACKED.

...JENSEN...
...LISTEN...
...YOU...

THOSE THINGS...
...THEY COULD HAVE KILLED US ALL...
...BUT THEY DIDN'T...
...THEY LET US GO...

OVER HERE!
WE NEED TO GET THIS MAN INSIDE RIGHT AWAY!
BRING A GURNEY-- A CHAIR!

...JENSEN...
...YOU HAVE TO...
NOT NOW, OWEN.
WE CAN TALK ABOUT THIS LATER.

YOU DON'T UNDERSTAND.
THIS PLACE...

EASY! EASY!

...THIS PLACE...

...THIS IS THE...

...LAST PLACE YOU NEED TO BE...

IS HE GOING TO BE ALL RIGHT?
HE IS, ISN'T HE?
THE DOCTORS CAN HELP HIM.

THEY'RE GOING TO HAVE QUESTIONS.
I KNOW.
THEY'RE GOING TO FIND OUT ABOUT MELISSA... ABOUT YOU.
I KNOW.

...WE HAVE RECEIVED EXCLUSIVE FOOTAGE FROM THE SCENE OF THE MOTEL DISTURBANCE.

BEFORE WE SHARE THIS WITH YOU, WE WANT TO OFFER A WARNING.
WHAT YOU ARE ABOUT TO SEE MAY DISTURB SOME VIEWERS.
KPPV
PARENTS MIGHT WANT TO HAVE THEIR CHILDREN LEAVE THE ROOM.
NEWS 24H
BREAKING NEWS
JONES 21045.28/ 56.19 /// NIKKEI 25159.51/ 17.11
MOTEL DISTU

WHAT ARE THEY--
THAT'S THE MOTEL.
THAT'S WHERE THEY CAME FOR US.

WE NEED TO GET THIS WRAPPED UP.
LAST THING WE NEED IS FOR SOMEONE TO CATCH A GLIMPSE OF...
...WHATEVER THE HELL THAT IS!
NEWS 24H
MOTEL DISTURBANCE
BREAKING NEWS
DOW JONES 21045.28/ 56.19 /// NIKKEI 25159.51/ 17.11 ///HANG SE

WE DO NOT HAVE CONFIRMATION OF WHAT WE ARE SEEING IN THIS VIDEO...
...BUT IT APPEARS TO BE SOME SORT OF...
...ALIEN LIFEFORM...

ALIEN?
IS THAT WHAT HE SAID?
CAN THAT BE REAL?

IT'S THE EMPTY MAN!
THAT'S WHAT THEY'RE SAYING!
THE EMPTY MAN...IT'S SOME SORT OF DAMN SPACE DISEASE...
...SENT HERE TO WEAKEN US BEFORE THE ALIENS COME!

WE NEED TO FIND SOMEPLACE SAFE.

KPPV
NEWS 24H
BREAKING
DISTURBANCE
...WE HAVE MADE INQUIRIES IN REGARDS TO HOW LONG THE AUTHORITIES HAVE KNOWN ABOUT THE EXISTENCE OF THESE CREATURES...
...AND WHY THIS INFORMATION HAS BEEN KEPT AWAY FROM THE PUBLIC...
...BUT WE HAVE RECEIVED NO COMMENT...

IT'S GOING TO GET WORSE.
SO MUCH WORSE.
THEY'RE GOING TO START A PANIC.

THEY'RE SENDING A MESSAGE.

WHERE ARE WE GOING TO GO?
WHERE WILL WE BE SAFE?
I DON'T KNOW.

I'LL DRIVE.
GIVE ME THE KEYS.
LOOK AFTER YOUR WIFE. I'LL BE FINE.

YOU WON'T.
YOU'RE SICK, JUST LIKE MELISSA.
I'M NOT GOING TO LET YOU DRIVE.

I DROVE US HERE.
GET IN THE CAR.

YOU'RE NOT DRIVING, AGENT JENSEN.
JUST HAND THE KEYS OVER.
YOU KNOW YOU'RE NOT ALL RIGHT.

YOU KNOW IT.
DAD--
ALL RIGHT, ALL RIGHT.
YOU WIN.
LET'S JUST-- GO.

I DON'T THINK I UNDER-STAND.
THIS WAS MY RIGHT.
MY HONOR.
IT WAS MY JOB TO SEND A MESSAGE TO THE EMPTY MAN.
OF COURSE, KARL. OF COURSE.
IT WAS YOUR RESPONSIBILITY.
AND YOU **FAILED.**
FAILED?
WE'VE HAD NATIONAL COVERAGE FOR THE LAST SEVERAL HOURS.
WE WOULD STILL BE AT THE TOP OF THE NEWS CYCLE IF NOT FOR YOUR LITTLE STUNT.
THAT STUNT, BY THE WAY, WAS THANKS TO MY EFFORTS.
THERE WOULDN'T HAVE BEEN A MANIFESTATION IF NOT FOR ME.
FINE, FINE.
AND WHAT DO YOU WANT NOW?
WHAT WOULD MAKE YOU HAPPY?
THE PLAYING FIELD HAS **EVOLVED,** KARL.
YOU'RE A BUSINESS MAN.
SURELY, YOU UNDERSTAND THAT.
YOU'VE BEEN MADE OBSOLETE BY RAPIDLY CHANGING TIMES.

OBSOLETE?
DO I NEED TO REMIND YOU WHAT I HAVE IN MY POSSESSION?
DO I NEED TO DETAIL THE TROUBLE I WENT THROUGH TO ACQUIRE IT?

CHANGING TIMES, KARL.
YOUR LITTLE TROPHY IS UNIMPORTANT NOW.
WE'VE **TRANSCENDED.**

YOU SHOULD BE HAPPY ABOUT THAT.
AT LEAST, YOU SHOULD IF YOU ARE TRULY FAITHFUL.
IF NOT, WELL--

SH-KRAK

MS. KINGSTON.
I'D LIKE YOU TO GATHER THE CONGREGATION ONCE MORE.
TELL THEM OUR WORK IS NOT DONE.

TELL THEM I NEED THEM FOR ANOTHER SHOW OF ***FAITH.***

WHERE ARE WE HEADING?

AGENT JENSEN?
ARE YOU LISTENING?
CAN YOU HEAR ME?

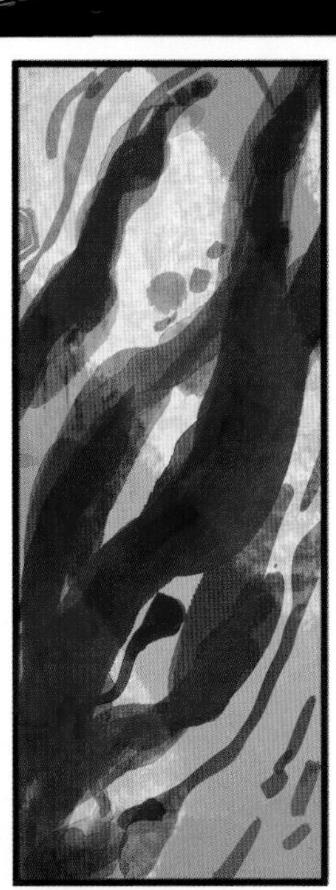

BA BAM BAM
SS·K·KK
I...
...I HEAR...
...I HEAR HIM...

NO!
GET AWAY!
STAY AWAY FROM THEM!
AAAH

SHE'S RIGHT.
THEY LET US GO.
IT WAS LIKE THEY **WANTED** US TO KILL ONE OF THEM.

WHAT ARE YOU TALKING ABOUT?

IT WAS A SACRIFICE.

YES!
YES! A SACRIFICE!
MOM?

WHEN WE KILLED ONE OF THEM...
...THEY JUST LEFT...
...LIKE THEY WANTED THAT...
...LIKE THEY KNEW IT WOULD BE REVEALED TO THE WORLD.

IT'S ALL...
...SO INSANE...
...IT MAKES NO DAMN SENSE...

THE EMPTY MAN ONLY WANTS TO BE HEARD.
HE WANTS MORE EYES AND EARS ON HIM...
ON HIS--

GOSPEL.

MELISSA, BABY...
...DON'T...
...JUST REST...

I DON'T KNOW WHAT YOUR GAME IS.
I DON'T KNOW WHAT YOU WANT FROM US.
BUT I KNOW YOU'RE NOT TRYING TO HELP US.

YOU'RE USING US.
YOU'RE USING MY WIFE.
YOU'RE TRYING TO PUNCH A HOLE INTO THE EMPTY MAN'S WORLD OR SOMETHING.
YOU SAID SO YOURSELF...YOU JUST WANT TO FIND YOUR PARTNER.

LANGFORD.
HE WAS GOING TO KILL THE EMPTY MAN IN HIS WORLD.
HE WAS GOING TO ASSASSINATE HIM...

"...BEFORE HE AWAKENED HERE."

AN MADE
RESTRICTED
AREA

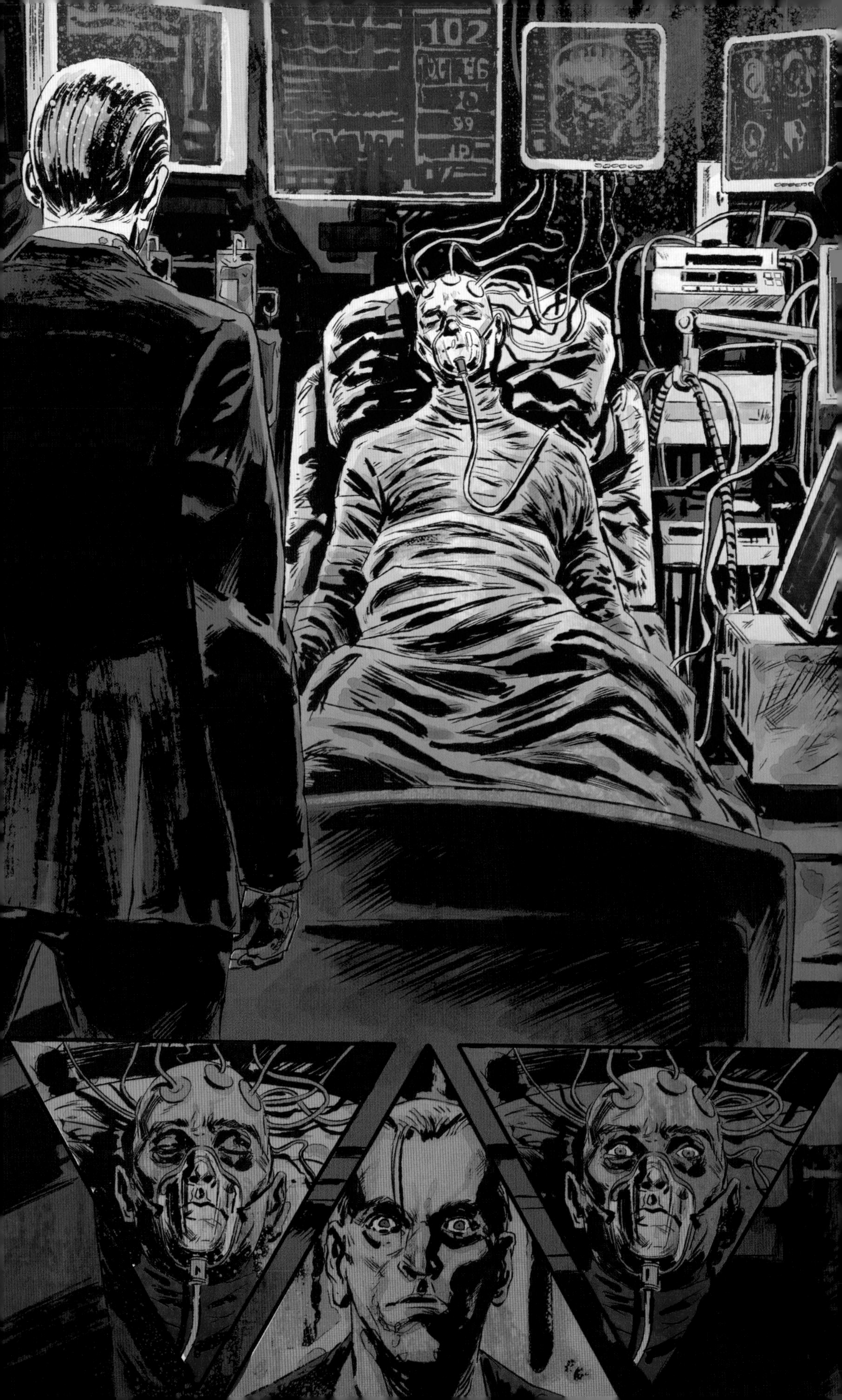
102

outside in

IT MADE ME

me DO IT

OR
LATER something

WASH the

CHAPTER TWO

"EVER SINCE THEY FOUND YOU, THEY'VE KEPT YOU HIDDEN.

"OR SO THEY THOUGHT.

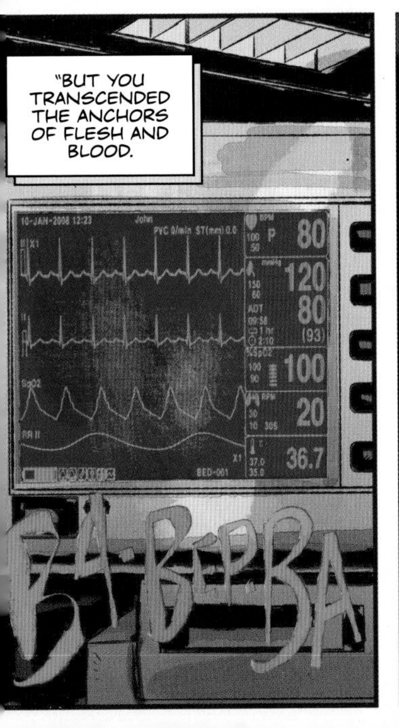
"BUT YOU TRANSCENDED THE ANCHORS OF FLESH AND BLOOD.

"I DOUBT SUCH PHYSICAL TRIVIALITIES *EVER* HAD A HOLD ON YOU.

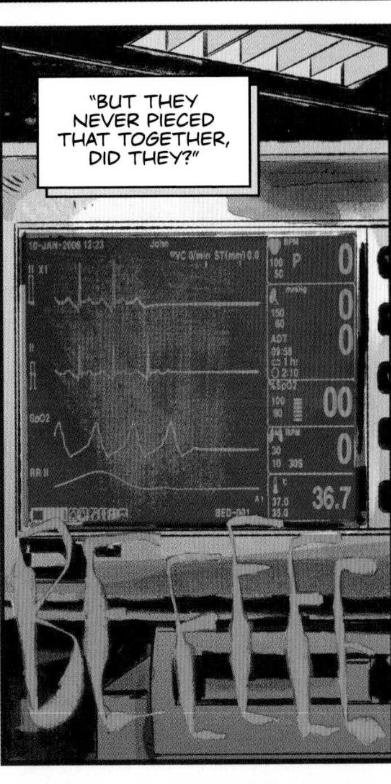
"BUT THEY NEVER PIECED THAT TOGETHER, DID THEY?"

HE'S FLATLINING!
WE NEED A FULL TEAM IN HERE--

WHU--

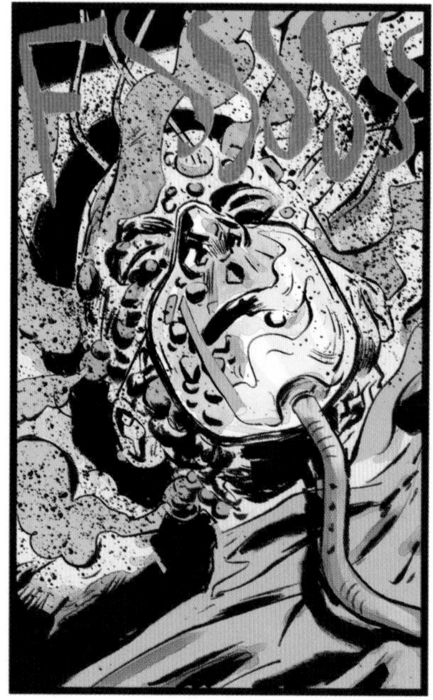

WHAT THE HELL?
WHAT JUST HAPPENED?
HOW--
IT'S ALL OVER ME!

WHAT IS THIS?
LIKE-- SPORES!
GOTTA GET THIS OFF OF ME!

KEEP CALM!
YOUR SUIT WILL PROTECT YOU FROM CONTAMINANTS.
YOU'LL BE FINE--
YOU DON'T UNDERSTAND!

I CAN HEAR HIM! HE'S TALKING TO ME!
EACH AND EVERY PARTICLE... SPEAKING TO ME... SCREAMING AT ME!
"BUT I UNDERSTOOD."

IT TOOK ME A WHILE TO FIGURE IT ALL OUT.

I SPENT MONTHS PLANNING ELABORATE ABDUCTION SCENARIOS.
I GATHERED FOLLOWERS.
I RECRUITED AGENTS WITHIN THE GOVERNMENT.
I STOCKPILED WEAPONS.

I INTENDED TO GO TO **WAR.**

WHAT ELSE COULD I DO?
GOD WAS BEING HELD PRISONER BY INFIDELS.
MY FAITH REQUIRED ACTION.

IT TOOK ME A WHILE TO FULLY UNDERSTAND WHAT YOU WERE TRYING TO TELL US.
IT'S NOT MY FAULT, REALLY.
LIKE EVERYONE ELSE, I'VE BEEN CONDITIONED TO BELIEVE ONLY IN WHAT I CAN SEE AND HEAR AND TOUCH.

FLESH IS MERELY PART OF THE EQUATION.
I DIDN'T NEED TO SEEK YOU OUT.
YOU WERE ALWAYS RIGHT HERE IN FRONT OF ME.

I BROUGHT THEM TO ME.
I GATHERED THOSE WHO COULD SEE YOU.
I BROUGHT THEM TOGETHER SO THEY COULD RE-MAKE YOU.

WE ARE ALL OF US THE EMPTY MAN.

SO YOU COULD BE REBORN.

I CALLED YOU BACK...

"...SO YOU COULD SEE THE WORLD WE HAVE MADE TOGETHER."
"...THE FEDERAL GOVERNMENT HAS DECLARED A STATE OF EMERGENCY...

"...WITH DANGEROUS RIOTS SPILLING OUT INTO THE STREETS...
"...FUELED, IT WOULD APPEAR, BY THE REVELATION THAT THE EMPTY MAN VIRUS HAS MUTATED...

"...AND THAT PHYSICAL MANIFESTATIONS OF THE DISEASE ARE APPEARING.

"MANY BELIEVE THAT THE GOVERNMENT HAS BEEN HIDING THE TRUTH...
"...THAT THE EXISTENCE OF THESE ALIEN BEINGS HAS BEEN HIDDEN FROM THE PUBLIC EYE UNTIL NOW...

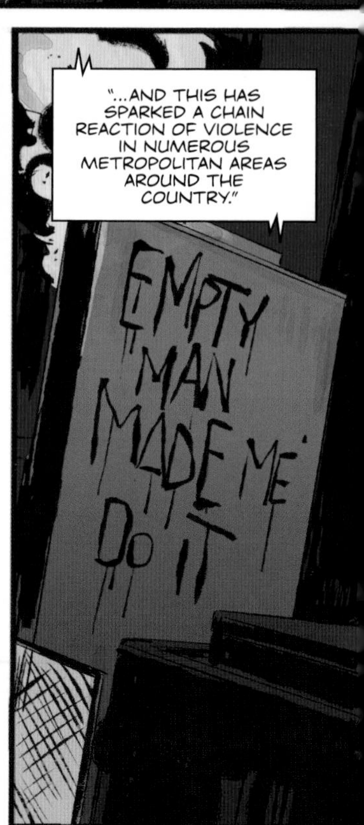
"...AND THIS HAS SPARKED A CHAIN REACTION OF VIOLENCE IN NUMEROUS METROPOLITAN AREAS AROUND THE COUNTRY."
EMPTY MAN MADE ME DO IT

"OFFICIALS ARE ADVISING CITIZENS TO STAY INSIDE."

DO NOT VENTURE OUTSIDE.

THE NATIONAL GUARD IS BEING MOBILIZED TO ASSIST THE POLICE AND EMERGENCY SERVICES...
...BUT IT WILL TAKE TIME TO CONTAIN THE ESCALATING VIOLENCE.

WE REPEAT, OFFICIALS ARE ADVISING THAT CITIZENS STAY IN THEIR HOMES WITH DOORS SECURED.
IF, HOWEVER, YOU SUSPECT A FRIEND OR FAMILY MEMBER OF SUFFERING FROM EMPTY MAN INFECTION, YOU SHOULD TAKE STEPS TO PROTECT YOURSELF.

FOR YOUR OWN DEFENSE, ARM YOURSELF WITH WHATEVER WEAPONS YOU HAVE ON HAND.

GUNS, KNIVES, BASEBALL BATS, ELECTRIC DRILLS, CHAINSAWS...
...ALL OF THESE THINGS ARE SUITABLE FOR HOME DEFENSE.

AND REMEMBER...

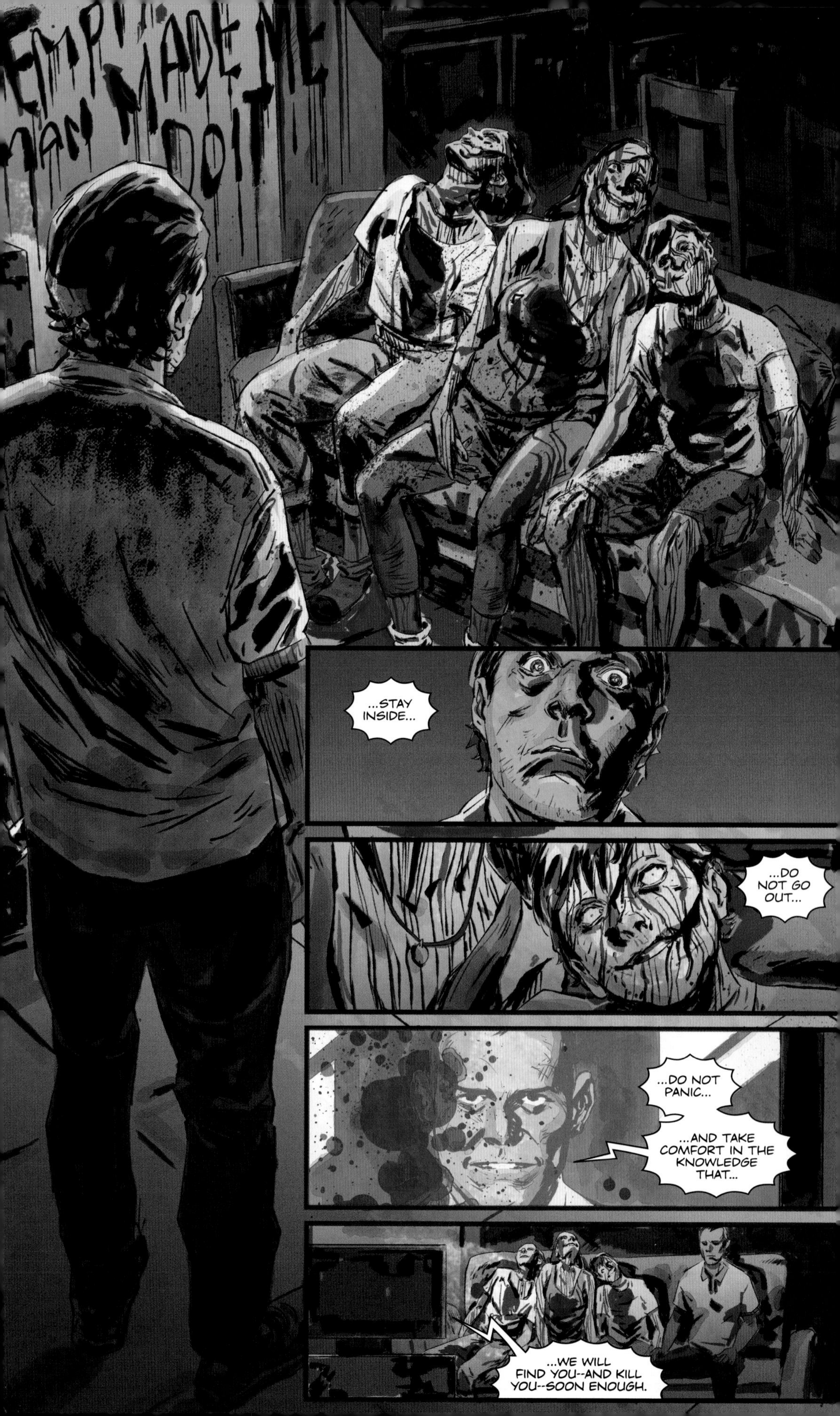
MADE ME
DO IT
...STAY INSIDE...
...DO NOT GO OUT...
...DO NOT PANIC...
...AND TAKE COMFORT IN THE KNOWLEDGE THAT...
...WE WILL FIND YOU--AND KILL YOU--SOON ENOUGH.

"LOOK AT THEM ALL."
BA
BEP
BEP
BA BA
BEE
BEP
HOW COULD THIS HAPPEN?
IS THIS ALL BECAUSE OF LEAKED IMAGES OF THOSE CREATURES?
HOW COULD IT ALL FALL APART SO QUICKLY?
QUICKLY?
ANDREW-- SOCIETY'S BEEN COLLAPSING SINCE THE DAY IT FIRST TOOK SHAPE.
THIS IS JUST THE ***NATURAL PROGRESSION.***
THIS IS IT, THEN?
IS IT OVER?
THIS IS HOW THE WORLD ENDS?
THIS IS HOW IT ***BEGINS.***
THIS IS WHAT THE EMPTY MAN WANTED ALL ALONG.
MASS CHAOS.
MASS INSANITY.

IT DOESN'T HAVE TO HURT.
WE ONLY SUFFER BECAUSE WE RESIST.
IF WE JUST ACCEPT WHAT'S COMING, WE'LL KNOW PEACE.
CAN WE STOP IT?
I DON'T KNOW.

IS THERE SOMEWHERE WE CAN GO?
SOME SORT OF SAFE ZONE?
A QUARANTINE--

DAD! A *QUARANTINE?*
WHAT DO YOU THINK WOULD HAPPEN TO MOM IF WE WENT SOMEWHERE LIKE THAT?
WE'VE BEEN PROTECTING HER FROM THAT ALL THIS TIME, AND NOW YOU JUST WANT TO ABANDON HER?

I DON'T KNOW WHAT ELSE TO DO, VICKI.
I CAN'T PROTECT YOUR MOTHER ANY LONGER.
BUT I MIGHT BE ABLE TO PROTECT YOU.

IT DOESN'T MATTER.
IT'S TOO LATE.
IT'S ALL COLLAPSING NOW.

WE'VE LOST.
"IS THERE ANYTHING YOU WOULD LIKE TO TELL OUR VIEWERS?"

A LOT OF PEOPLE ARE AFRAID RIGHT NOW.
THERE ARE...EVENTS TAKING PLACE OUT IN THE WORLD...
...TERRIFYING EVENTS...

...THAT SEEM TO BE CONNECTED TO THE EMPTY MAN...

...SO IS THERE SOMETHING YOU WANT TO SAY TO GIVE PEOPLE SOME SENSE OF COMFORT?

YES.

BEWARE.

BEWARE FALSE PROPHETS.

NOW, MORE THAN EVER.
THERE ARE THOSE WHO WILL TRICK YOU.
THERE ARE THOSE WHO WILL BETRAY YOU.

THEY WILL MAKE PROMISES ON BEHALF OF THE EMPTY MAN.

THIS IS HOW WE WILL ALL BE TESTED.

"YOU MUST TRUST IN YOURSELF ABOVE ALL OTHERS...
"...FOR YOU ARE THE EMPTY MAN."

GOD.

"KNOW THAT WHEN YOU SEE THE WORLD OF THE EMPTY MAN...

"...YOU WILL SEE IT THROUGH YOUR OWN EYES."

KRAA-SMASH

OH MY GOD!
DID YOU SEE THAT!
HE JUST HIT--

HONK-KRASH

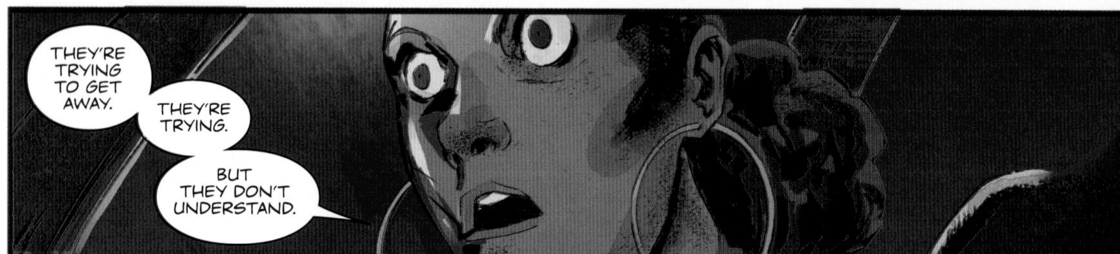
THEY'RE TRYING TO GET AWAY.
THEY'RE TRYING.
BUT THEY DON'T UNDERSTAND.

SKRRR-SNASH

THEY NEED HELP!
SOMEONE COULD BE HURT!
PROBABLY IS HURT!
DON'T GO OUT THERE.

DAD--YOU'LL GET YOURSELF RUN OVER!

HE HEARS...
...HEARS METAL UPON METAL...
...LIKE BELLS CALLING...

WE CAN'T STAY HERE.

SPLUT!

SSKRRR
GO!
ANDREW-- GO!
WE HAVE TO GET OUT OF HERE!
W-WHERE? HOW?
IT'S BUMPER TO--

SSSKREEEEEEE

DAD!
PLEASE--

VFFF

VRRRRR

KRASMASH

EVERYONE--
HOLD ON!

VRAVRRR

SSKK
VRRRRRRRR

SKKKKKKR
AH--
VRRRRR

SKKKKKKK
VRRRR

SKKKK

VRRRRR

ARE YOU ALL RIGHT?
IS EVERYONE OK?

I--
I THINK SO.

WE NEED TO...
...WE HAVE TO FIGURE OUT...

WRRR

SKEEEE

SKAK
AAAUUUGH!
DAD!

SLAM

NNNNN--

HEY!
HEY!
OVER HERE!

LEAVE THEM ALONE!
HSSSK
YOU WANT SOMEONE?
I'M RIGHT HERE!

HSSSSS
I'M RIGHT--

KA-BAM

I--

LANGFORD?
HEY THERE, JENSEN.
LONG TIME, NO SEE.
LOOKS LIKE THE WORLD'S KIND OF GONE DOWNHILL WHILE I WAS AWAY.

outside IN

IT MADE ME

Me DO It

OR

LATER SOMETHIN

LL WASH the

CHAPTER THREE

"THE EMPTY MAN NO LONGER NEEDED FLESH AND BLOOD.
"HE HAD TRANSCENDED.
"HE HAD BECOME A BEING OF PURE MENTAL ENERGY.
"IN OUR WORLD, HE MIGHT SPREAD OUT.
"BUT ON THE OTHER SIDE, HE WAS ANCHORED.
"I THOUGHT IF I COULD FIND HIM, I COULD KILL HIM.
"I THOUGHT I COULD END THIS ONCE AND FOR ALL.
"ONCE AND FOR ALL."

"IT STRUCK ME AS ODD...
"...FOR A 'GOD' WHO DIDN'T NEED FLESH...
"...THE ONLY WAY TO REACH HIM WAS THROUGH SKIN AND MUSCLE AND FLESH AND BLOOD.
"IT WAS LIKE BEING **BORN.**

"BORN INTO HELL.
"GAZING OUT ACROSS THE LANDSCAPE FOR THE FIRST TIME, I ALMOST GAVE UP HOPE.
"ALMOST."

"MAYBE...IF I'M BEING HONEST...PASSING THROUGH THAT DOOR IN THE FIRST PLACE WAS GIVING UP.
"IT'S NOT LIKE I HAD MUCH TIME ON THE OTHER SIDE.
"I WAS SICK.
"DYING.

"MAYBE I STILL WAS.
"WE ALL ARE, AREN'T WE?"

"IN ONE WAY OR ANOTHER.
"I WALKED FOR DAYS.
"DAYS...AND I NEVER SAW ANOTHER LIVING SOUL.
"THERE WERE SIGNS, THOUGH...
"...EVIDENCE THAT I WAS NOT THE FIRST TO COME TO THIS PLACE...
"...THAT OTHERS HAD COME HERE, HOPING TO KILL THE EMPTY MAN...
"...THAT OTHERS HAD FAILED."

BUT I KEPT ON SEARCHING FOR HIM.

YOU NEVER FOUND HIM.
YOU WERE GONE SO LONG.
BUT YOU NEVER FOUND THE EMPTY MAN.

I DIDN'T SAY THAT.

WH-WHAT ARE THOSE... THINGS?

I TOLD YOU I WAS SICK.
THOSE THINGS...
...THEY'RE PART OF ME, I GUESS.
THEY'RE MY DISEASE.
I WAS ALONE.
I WAS OUT THERE...IN THE WILDS OF THE EMPTY MAN'S MIND.
AND I WAS ALONE.
AND ONE DAY I JUST...
...PUKED THEM UP...
...AND I WASN'T ALONE ANYMORE.
HOW DID YOU FEEL THEN?

I FELT...
...EMPTY.
SO, YOU DID FIND HIM?
YOU FOUND THE EMPTY MAN.
WHAT HAPPENED?
JENSEN...
UH--
WE HAVE COMPANY.

WE NEED TO MOVE.

WE NEED TO FIND A CAR THAT RUNS.
A CLEAR ROADWAY.

EVEN IF WE CAN JUST TRAVEL A FEW MILES AT A TIME--

WHERE WILL WE GO?
LANGFORD-- YOU'RE NOT ANSWERING MY QUESTIONS.
HOW DID YOU FIND US?
WHAT HAPPENED WHEN YOU FOUND THE EMPTY MAN?

YOU'VE ALWAYS BEEN AN *ANCHOR* FOR ME.
I'VE ALWAYS KNOWN WHERE YOU WERE, EVEN WHEN I WAS STUCK IN THAT OTHER PLACE.
AND AS FOR THE EMPTY MAN...
...I'M LOOKING AT HIM.

...THERE'S NO DENYING THAT THE SITUATION HAS GROWN SIGNIFICANTLY MORE DANGEROUS.
WE MUST HOLD OURSELVES ACCOUNTABLE FOR THIS ESCALATION.
WHAT ARE YOU SUGGESTING? THAT THE MEDIA IS TO BLAME?
ARE WE SUPPOSED TO SIMPLY STAY QUIET ABOUT WHAT IS HAPPENING IN THE WORLD?
THE PUBLIC HAS A RIGHT TO KNOW WHAT'S HAPPENING.

CERTAINLY, CERTAINLY.
BUT WE HAVE A GREAT RESPONSIBILITY IN TERMS OF OUR MESSAGING.
THERE ARE NETWORKS THAT ARE PRESENTING AN ALMOST APOCALYPTIC VIEW OF WHAT IS HAPPENING.

LOOK OUT THE WINDOW!
THIS **IS** THE APOCALYPSE!

ONLY BECAUSE WE WANT IT TO BE.
SINCE THE EARLIEST DAYS OF THIS CRISIS, CULTS HAVE BEEN FORMING.
NOW, MASS MEDIA HAS, ITSELF, BECOME ONE OF THESE CULTS.

WE ARE THE EMPTY MAN'S PROPHETS.

AND WE ALL KNOW THERE ARE
SSKKZZZK
WHO BELIEVE ANYTHING
KZZZZZK
SEE BROADCASTED--

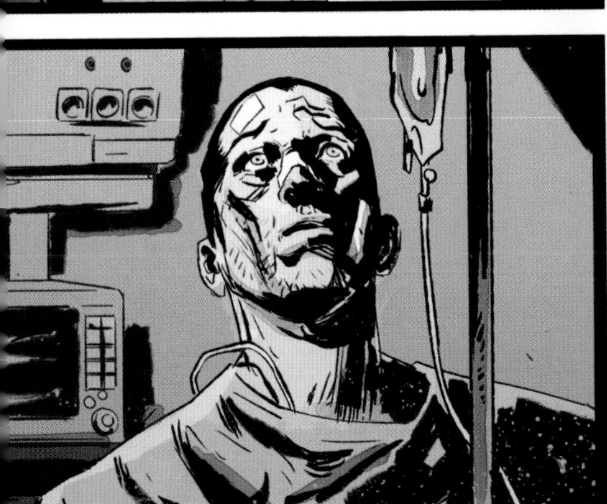

J-JENSEN--

MR. MARSH!
WHAT ARE YOU DOING OUT OF BED?
THAT'S SIMPLY UNACCEPTABLE FOR A MAN IN YOUR CONDITION!

WHATEVER ARE WE GOING TO DO WITH YOU?
NNN--
NNGEEEEAAAA
THE EMPTY MAN MADE ME DO IT.

AH, KARL.
I SEE YOU DECIDED NOT TO LISTEN.

YOU HAVE NO PLACE HERE.
I KNOW IT'S PAINFUL, BUT YOU ARE NO LONGER ESSENTIAL TO OUR PLANS.
IT WOULD BE BEST IF YOU TURNED AROUND NOW...

...BEFORE YOU EMBARRASS YOURSELF FURTHER.

YOU KNOW WHO THIS IS.
YOU KNOW WHAT I HAVE RAISED.
DO YOU TRULY INTEND TO TURN ME AWAY?
TO TURN *HIM* AWAY?

YOU DO NOT UNDERSTAND.
YOUR FAITH IS STRONG BUT MISGUIDED.
YOU BRING US A BLADE OF GRASS...

"...WHILE THE EMPTY MAN GROWS LIKE A SPRAWLING GARDEN."
WE'RE NOT GOING TO MAKE IT OUT OF THIS.
THERE'S NO WAY, IS THERE?
WE'RE NOT GOING TO SURVIVE.
THIS IS THE END.
NOT YET.

"THE EMPTY MAN DOESN'T WANT AN APOCALYPSE.
"QUITE THE OPPOSITE, IN FACT.
"IT TOOK ME A WHILE TO FULLY UNDERSTAND IT.
"HE DIDN'T WANT TO DESTROY.
"HE WANTED TO CREATE.
"HE WANTED TO BUILD SOMETHING HARMONIOUS AND PEACEFUL.
"BUT IT ALL TURNED SO UGLY.
"HE DREW THE MINDS OF OTHERS INTO HIS OWN...
"...CONSUMED AND PROCESSED THEM..."

"...AND HIS MIND SIMPLY CRAPPED OUT EVERYTHING IT DIDN'T USE.
"GARBAGE IN, GARBAGE OUT.

"THE EMPTY MAN HAS ALWAYS BEEN WITH US.
"THE FIRST BIT OF INDEPENDENT THOUGHT WE EVER EXPERIENCED--THAT WAS HUMANITY'S FIRST TASTE OF INSANITY.
"NAMING IT--CALLING IT THE EMPTY MAN--THAT WAS THE LAST.
"WE THOUGHT IF WE NAMED IT, WE MIGHT HAVE SOME SEMBLANCE OF CONTROL OVER IT.
"THAT'S HOW IT'S ALWAYS BEEN."

HAVE YOU COME TO KILL ME?
AT LONG LAST, HAVE YOU COME?
I'VE BEEN *EXPECTING* YOU...
...OR *REMEMBERING* THIS ENCOUNTER...
...AND I WELCOME YOU.
YOU'RE NOT GOING TO STOP ME?
SHOULD I?
SO MANY HAVE COME BEFORE YOU.
WHEN I CAME HERE, I WAS BLINDED AND CONFUSED, TOO.
I WANTED TO BE A GOD.
INSTEAD, I BECAME A *DISEASE.*

YOU REALIZE, OF COURSE, THAT YOU ARE DYING.
YOU WERE DECAYING AND ROTTING IN THE "REAL" WORLD.
BUT HERE YOU ARE WELL.
WHEN YOU KILL ME, WILL YOU FALL ILL ONCE MORE?
WILL YOUR TUMORS TURN ON YOU?
WILL THEY EAT YOU ALIVE?
WE'RE ABOUT TO FIND OUT.
I LIKE YOU.
I LOOK FORWARD TO HAVING THIS TALK AGAIN.
BLAAAM
"I KILLED HIM."

AND IT CHANGED NOTHING.

YOU'RE WRONG.
EVERYTHING'S CHANGED.
FOR THE WORSE, LANGFORD.

WE WERE BOTH **SO WRONG.**

NO.
WE CAN STOP THIS.
WE CAN KILL THE EMPTY MAN ONCE AND FOR ALL.
BUT...

BUT WHAT?
IF WE CAN SET THINGS RIGHT, WE HAVE TO TRY.
EVEN IF THERE ARE RISKS.

IT'S NOT A RISK. IT'S A ***CERTAINTY.***
THERE'S A WAY TO KILL THE EMPTY MAN.
IF WE DO IT, THOUGH, WE END THE WORLD WITH HIM.

"HE SAID IT HIMSELF.
"HE WANTED TO BE A GOD.
"HE **ASCENDED** INTO MADNESS.
"HE WAS JUST **ONE OF MANY** WHO HAD DONE SO."
HAVE YOU COME TO KILL ME?
AT LONG LAST, HAVE YOU COME?
I'VE BEEN **EXPECTING** YOU...
...OR **REMEMBERING** THIS ENCOUNTER...
...AND I WELCOME YOU.
WHAT IS--
"WE DIDN'T CREATE THE EMPTY MAN IN OUR OWN IMAGE..."

"...BUT ONCE WE SAW HIM, WE WANTED TO **CO-OPT** HIS **DIVINITY**.
"WE THOUGHT IF HE COULD DO IT, WHY NOT US?
"THOUSANDS OF GODS, BORN SCREAMING INTO HEAVEN AND HELL.
"ALL WANTING PEACE AND UNITY.
"ALL TEARING ONE ANOTHER APART TO GET IT.
"ALL OF US BROADCASTING.
"WE ARE--EVERY LAST LIVING SOUL--THE EMPTY MAN."

outside IN

IT MADE ME IT

ME DO IT

OR

LATER SOMETHIN

ILL WASH THE

CHAPTER FOUR

NOBODY KNOWS WHO FIRST COINED THE TERM "**THE EMPTY MAN.**"
TERRORISTS PROCLAIMING THEIR OWN NOTORIETY.

PHARMACEUTICAL COMPANIES PUSHING PILLS.

RELIGIOUS WHACK-JOBS PRAYING FOR AN APOCALYPSE.

THE TRUTH IS, WE HAVE NO IDEA.

SOME SAY THE DISEASE NAMED ITSELF.
IT INFECTED US LONG AGO...
...WITH THE FIRST **FLICKER** OF COGNIZANCE...
...AND IT HAS BEEN INCUBATING FOR ALL THIS TIME.
THERE HAVE BEEN FLARE-UPS ALONG THE WAY.
WAR AND GENOCIDE.
THE FOUNDING OF POLITICAL AND RELIGIOUS SYSTEMS.
FOR THE MOST PART, THOUGH, THE DISEASE HAS BIDED ITS TIME.
"THE DISEASE."

WHILE THE WORLD **PERSONIFIES** THE MADNESS, I'M STILL TRYING TO **DEHUMANIZE** IT.

THAT'S HOW THE EMPTY MAN HAS SURVIVED SO LONG.
W-WHY?
WHY WOULD YOU HOLD US BACK?
WHY WOULD YOU CALL US AND THEN K-KEEP US OUT?
HOLD THEM BACK!
THEY'RE TRYING TO GET IN!
STOP THEM!
TOO MANY!
THERE'S TOO MANY OF THEM!
WE NEED BACKUP!

THIS IS IT.
THIS IS OUR MOMENT.
WE'RE GOING IN.
H-HOW?
EVEN IF WE GET PAST THE GUARDS...PAST ALL THOSE PEOPLE...
...THE BUILDING WILL BE LOCKED UP TIGHT.
I'LL SHOW YOU.

IT'S NOT BUDGING.

W-WHAT DID I SAY?
I TOLD YOU.
WE NEED TO GET OUT OF HERE.
IF THEY F-FIND US...

SHS-KLICK

H-HOW--?
A CHURCH IS MOST AFRAID OF THE FAITHFUL.

WHAT HAPPENED TO YOU OVER THERE, LANGFORD?
WHAT DID YOU SEE ON THE OTHER SIDE?
YOU'RE **DIFFERENT.**
THAT'S JUST IT, JENSEN.
I'M NOT.
NONE OF US ARE--

cof! cof!

I DIDN'T MISS THAT.
YOU'RE SICK AGAIN.
NOW THAT YOU'VE RETURNED...

...YOUR CANCER'S COME BACK.

WE'RE GOING TO KILL HIM, MONICA.
YOU AND ME.
WE'RE GOING TO KILL THE EMPTY MAN.

YOU SAID THAT WOULD END THE WORLD.

YEAH.
BUT JUST IMAGINE.
JUST IMAGINE WHAT COMES **NEXT.**

WHAT NOW?
NOW THAT WE'RE HERE...
...WHAT ARE WE GOING TO DO?

WE STOP THE SIGNAL.

THE BUILDING'S BEEN BREACHED.
WE NEED TO KEEP YOU SAFE.
WE NEED TO GET YOU TO A SECURE LOCATION.
WE CAN REACH THE PARKING GARAGE...
...GET YOU CLEAR...
...RUN RIGHT OVER THEM IF WE NEED TO.
IT'S ALL FALLING APART.
THIS IS WHAT YOU WANTED. BUT NOT LIKE THIS.
YOU UNDERESTIMATED HOW QUICKLY IT WOULD ESCALATE.
AND NOW YOU NEED ME--NEED *HIM*--ONCE THE SIGNAL IS BROKEN.
I UNDERESTIMATED NOTHING, KARL.
YOU, THOUGH.
WHAT DO YOU THINK *YOU'RE* BECOMING?
DO YOU THINK YOU'RE A PRIEST?
YOU'RE JUST ANOTHER **GOAT.**
CRRRR

COME, CHILDREN.

HSSSSSSS
BLAM
AHH--
BLAM
BLAM
BLAM
BLAM
RREAUU
LANGFORD--
I'M ALL RIGHT.
IT'S...
...OVER.
3
3
3

SORRY FOR THE MESS.
BUT WE NEED TO HAVE A WORD.
WE NEED TO SET THINGS RIGHT.

WHO--

WE KNOW YOU.
YOU WERE THERE.
WHEN WE CAME BACK.

YOU REMEMBER.

WHAT DO YOU WANT?

WE WANT TO STOP THE BROADCAST.
WE WANT TO KILL IT.
WE WANT TO KILL THE EMPTY MAN.

Y-YOU CAN'T STOP THE BROADCAST.
NOT NOW.
AND I WON'T LET YOU HARM--
3
BAM
I THINK MAYBE...
...MAYBE SHE BELIEVED IN WHAT SHE WAS DOING...
...SHE BELIEVED YOU TWO WERE JUST A COUPLE OF KIDS...
...SHE BELIEVED...
...JUST LIKE WE DID.
LANGFORD! WHAT ARE YOU DOING?
SHE WAS UNARMED!
THEY'RE JUST CHILDREN!
NO.
NO, JENSEN.
THOSE DRUGS OF YOURS MUST BE WEARING OFF BY NOW.

LOOK AGAIN.
SEE THEM FOR WHAT THEY ARE.
SEE THEM AS THE REST OF THE WORLD SEES THEM.
THEY'RE MESSENGERS.
DISCIPLES.
HSSSSSSSSSSK
THEY'RE PREACHING THE EMPTY MAN'S GOSPEL.
KAFF! HGGK!
3
3

THEY CAN SHOW US THE WAY.

THEY'LL STOP US.
THEY'LL--
THEY WON'T.
YOU SEE THEM NOW.
YOU SEE THEM FOR WHAT THEY ARE.
AND THEY SEE YOU.

WAIT!
WHAT ARE YOU DOING?
YOU SAID YOU COULD STOP THIS!
YOU CAN'T JUST ABANDON US HERE!
ABANDONED.
THAT'S AN INTERESTING CHOICE OF WORDS.
I'M SORRY FOR WHAT'S HAPPENED TO YOUR FAMILY.
I'M SORRY FOR WHAT WILL HAPPEN NEXT.

THIS IS...
A TEMPLE.
AN EMPTY TEMPLE.
ABANDONED.
WHY ARE WE HERE?
THE EMPTY MAN WASN'T A PERSON.
NOT INITIALLY.
IT WAS A *THOUGHT*.
I DON'T KNOW IF THE THOUGHT WAS BORN FROM A PERSON'S MIND...
...OR IF IT JUST SPRUNG TO LIFE...
...BUT EVENTUALLY, SOMEONE--A CREATURE OF FLESH AND BLOOD--LATCHED ONTO IT AND TOOK CONTROL.
NOT THAT A THOUGHT CAN BE CONTROLLED.
BUT THAT PERSON COULDN'T STAY HERE FOREVER.
THEY LEFT THIS PLACE.
THEY LEFT A VOID.
"PRETENDERS CAME ALONG.
"THEY TRIED TO BECOME THE EMPTY MAN.
"THEY FORMED DENOMINATIONS OF INSANITY."

YOUR CANCER--
HGG
YOU CAME BACK TO OUR WORLD TO GET ME.
YOU WANTED ME TO TAKE THE EMPTY MAN'S PLACE.
YOU WANTED ME TO STOP THE BROADCAST.

EVEN IF I STOP THE SIGNAL, THOUGH...
...THE OTHERS...
...THE PRETENDERS...

I NEED MY SICKNESS TO RETURN.
"YOU ARE GOD NOW..."

...AND GOD NEEDS AN *ARMY OF ANGELS.*
GO FORTH.
HUNT THE PRETENDERS.
MURDER THEM.
THE WORLD...OUR WORLD...WON'T MAKE IT.
ONLY THE SANE WILL SURVIVE.
AND THERE JUST AREN'T THAT MANY OF THEM OUT THERE.
THEN I WILL BRING THOSE WE CAN INTO THIS WORLD.
MY WORLD.
IT IS, AFTER ALL, TOO *EMPTY.*

"BUT THE BROADCASTS--ALL OF THEM--MUST BE STOPPED."
I CAN'T HEAR! I CAN'T SEE!
WHY?
WHY HAVE YOU FORSAKEN US?
WE MADE THE EMPTY MAN! DO IT
M-MOM?
ARE YOU ALL RIGHT?
MOM?
WHAT IS IT?

THEY ARE SHUTTING IT DOWN.
THEY ARE SHUTTING DOWN PART OF THE WORLD.
IT'S THE **FLOOD.**
IT'S THE **FLAME.**
THE **RAPTURE.**
BUT THERE ARE SO MANY OTHERS.
SO MANY EMPTY MEN.
OH, VICKI.
THEY'RE STARTING A HOLY WAR.
IT WILL BE FOUGHT IN THE EMPTY MAN'S WORLD...
...AND IN THIS ONE.
AND THAT'S HOW IT STARTED.
NOT THE END OF THE WORLD.
BUT THE BEGINNING OF THE WAR.
WE DIDN'T WANT TO BE SOLDIERS.
WE DIDN'T WANT TO FIGHT.
BUT THE EMPTY MAN MADE US DO IT.

outside IN

IT MADE ME

me DO IT

OR LATER SOMETHIN

WASH the

ISSUE FIVE COVER BY **VANESA R. DEL REY**

ISSUE FIVE COVER BY JESÚS HERVÁS

ISSUE SIX COVER BY **VANESA R. DEL REY**

ISSUE SIX COVER BY JESÚS HERVÁS

ISSUE SEVEN COVER BY VANESA R. DEL REY

ISSUE SEVEN COVER BY JESÚS HERVÁS

ISSUE EIGHT COVER BY VANESA R. DEL REY

ISSUE EIGHT COVER BY JESÚS HERVÁS

CULLEN BUNN

writes graphic novels, comic books, short fiction, and novels. He has written The Sixth Gun, The Damned, Helheim, and The Tooth for Oni Press; Harrow County for Dark Horse; The Empty Man, The Unsound, and Bone Parish for BOOM! Studios; Dark Ark, Unholy Grail, and Brothers Dracul for AfterShock Comics; and Regression and Cold Spots for Image Comics. He also writes titles such as Asgardians of the Galaxy and numerous Deadpool series for Marvel Comics.

JESÚS HERVÁS

is a cartoonist and illustrator from Madrid, father of two little tornado girls, almost forest engineer, and judoka, in addition to more things that aren't as cool. Before joining Cullen Bunn to portray the horror in The Empty Man, Jesús has drawn series such as Clive Barker's Hellraiser, Sons of Anarchy, and Kurt Sutter's Lucas Stand for BOOM! Studios and Penny Dreadful for Titan, as well as albums Deluge and Androids for the French publisher Soleil.

NIKO GUARDIA

is a colorist and animation artist working out of Northampton, Massachusetts. He has been coloring comic books professionally since 2013 for BOOM! Studios, Image, and Black Mask on titles such as Hit 1957, Dead Letters, The Empty Man, Come Into Me, and The Gravediggers Union. His animation credits include shows on Adult Swim, Disney, and Nickelodeon. He also is the co-creator of the animation collective, Todo Todo. He doesn't have any cats.

ED DUKESHIRE

Born in Seoul, Korea, Ed Dukeshire is a graphic artist and Harvey-nominated comic book letterer who has worked in the biz since 2001. He has lettered titles from mainstream to creator-owned favorites. He also owns and operates the Digital Webbing website, a gathering place for comic creators. And you may even catch him playing video games once in a while.